You've Got E-Meoww!!!

Susan Carleson Currer

PAGE PUBLISHING
Conneaut Lake, PA

First originally published by Page Publishing 2024

ISBN 979-8-89157-389-5 (pbk)
ISBN 979-8-89157-265-2 (hc)
ISBN 979-8-89157-248-5 (digital)

Printed in the United States of America

This book is dedicated to
my beloved Nougat,
Peanut, Chester, Arthur,
Tommy and Emily Kate —
forever in my heart.

Foreword

Those of us fortunate enough to share our lives with a *Felis domesticus* know they communicate in many ways. For centuries they have charmed and controlled us by crying, chirping, chattering, clawing, climbing, purring, scratching, singing and staring — oh, that look they give you! We have grown accustomed to their devices, and we have learned from them how to conduct ourselves in their presence (well, for the most part).

My cat is an indoor cat. He was an outdoor cat, but with the arrival of *Black Bart* in our neighborhood and the ensuing veterinarian bills, *Nougat* moved inside. I noticed at once a change in him. No longer able to communicate with his own preferred species, he became much more interested in communicating with me. His favorite method was to help me with my correspondence on the computer. As soon as he would hear the clicking of the keys, he'd be on my lap and then gingerly up onto the desk where he would wind himself back and forth across the keyboard.

One day, *Nougat* didn't wait for me. He had watched closely and learned how to do it himself. He had invented *E-MEOWW.* This book is a compilation of correspondence between *Nougat* and his favorite nephew *Arbogast.* (While I was aware that *Nougat* was a "lap-top-kitty" I had no idea that he had so much to say.)

Nougat and I believe that *E-MEOWW* will revolutionize the lives of indoor cats everywhere — well, at least those with access to a modem. The following communiqués depict actual events and points of view and have been translated to provide for easier reading.

When I sit down to

compose my prose,

I lick my paws

then wipe my nose;

I stretch my legs

to wash my toes.

Boy, time sure flies—

Time for a doze...

by Nougat

Greetings Nephew

From: Nougat **Nougat@e-meoww.com**
To: Arbogast **Arbogast@e-meoww.com**

Dear Arbogast,

You've been on my mind lately. You're not a kitten anymore, and I think the time has come for your Uncle Nougat to give you some advice on getting control of your household. I've had a lot of experience I can share with you to maximize your happiness. Remember—

> Life is only as good as your skill in getting **what** you want **when** you want it!

Establishing who's in charge of a household is never easy, but with perseverance and good advice (that's where I come in), in time you should be able to handle your humans with the best of us. ***Your worldview vs. theirs.***

Take your food bowl for instance. Your folks are likely to see it as half full when it's really half empty! You can help them understand that this will not do by tipping the bowl over. This is most effective if you can flip it so the kibble scatters all over the floor and under the major appliances. This makes quite an impression and along with the fun of seeing them on their hands and knees trying to scoop the stuff up, the odd bit that they miss makes excellent bait for mousies or even a good juicy beetle. (I do not recommend this technique with your water bowl — trust me.)

Hey kid, I gotta run now — catch ya later!

Your favorite uncle,
Nougat

Hi Uncle Nougat

From: Arbogast   **Arbogast@e-meoww.com**
To: Nougat   **Nougat@e-meoww.com**

Dear Uncle Nougat,

Thanks for the e-meoww. It's my first letter I ever got. You're right about me not being a kitten anymore. I'm not growing as fast as I'd like to though — my little sister Lucie is catching up fast! But what I lack in size I make up for in attitude! I will **NOT** be bossed around or ignored! Just ask my folks. The other day Lucie tried to take over. She walks up to me, right? Then she sits down in front of me with her face right up to mine — are you following this? Then she slowly, I mean **slooooowly,** raises her paw up to the side of my face. I stayed cool though, and just stared at her. Then she lowers her paw.
Then she raises her paw again — right up to my face so
close I could almost feel it! Then she lowers it again —
up and down, up and down. She practically gave me a
nervous breakdown 'cause I knew I couldn't flinch.

Finally, she raises her paw one last time and then the
silly idiot freaked out and ran down the hall and hid
under the bed. Can you believe it?
I was rattled but I kept my cool and I'm still
THE BOSS.

Hey, Uncle Nougat, are you a guy or a
girl, or what? I hope you're a guy like
me. But even if you aren't I hope you'll
keep writing to me.

Meow for now,
Arbo

We Guys Got to Stick Together

From: Nougat   **Nougat@e-meoww.com**
To: Arbogast **Arbogast@e-meoww.com**

Dear Arbo,

When I was your age I had a tough attitude, too. But you know, as I got older I discovered that you get lots more out of life if people like you than if they're scared of you. You get tons more lap time if they know you won't scratch. Just keep that in mind.

Now, getting to your question about my gender. I am a guy. I wasn't always a guy — I mean, my mom thought I was a girl when I first moved in. (Maybe that explains my name?) Oh well, after a few months I started getting beaten up by a real bully called ***Black Bart***. My mom used to chase him out of the yard, but not before I could catch him and clobber him. Only he was a lot better at clobbering me, so one day he got me good and my mom took me to ***The Vet***. I don't know if you've ever been to ***The Vet*** but let me warn ya —

Keep your eye on him and ***do not let him lift up your tail!***

Anyway, after the doc checked me out and bandaged me up, he said to my mom that her little "princess" was in fact a prince. I guess I must have been broken once because my mom says I've been "fixed."

Gotta run nephew,
Uncle Nougat

It's a Guy Thing

From: Arbogast **Arbogast@e-meoww.com**
To: Nougat **Nougat@e-meoww.com**

Dear Uncle Nougat,

I'm glad to hear that you're a guy like me. I think it's
easier to relate to another guy. Take my dad for instance.
Every morning when he gets up he goes into the room with the
waterfall and he cleans himself. Have you noticed how much easier
we cats have it — we can wash ourselves **ANYPLACE** we want to —
and I think we generally do a better job, but where was I?

Oh yeah, he stands in front of this funny window that has another
dad on the other side of it looking back at him — do you know what
I'm talking about here? Anyway, I jump up on the side of the sink and
watch while he takes this noisy box and he rubs it over his face. It
takes his whiskers off! I'd hate to lose **MY** whiskers —
but he takes his off every morning! Can you believe it?

Anyhow, I hope this message finds you fat and furry. Well, not too
fat, but certainly furry. I am (furry, not fat).

Your favorite nephew,
Arbogast

A Hunting I Will Go!

From: Arbogast   **Arbogast@e-meoww.com**
To: Nougat   **Nougat@e-meoww.com**

Dear Uncle Nougat,

Hey Uncle Nougat, I went hunting last night! Well, kind of. There was this spider up on the ceiling, see? I couldn't take my eyes off him. Anywhere he went up there, I followed on the floor.

First, I jumped up on the couch, figuring I could jump up and get him. **WRONG!** So, I jumped up onto the dresser — I'm up pretty high now! I waited, just watching as he came closer... here he comes, just walkin'... and then just as I'm ready to reach up and grab him my dad grabs **ME**! He said something about spiders being "bad protein" whatever that means.

Anyway, I thought about it all night and I figure I'll get another chance one of these days and I'll be ready.

Hey, I think I see somethin' in the corner! Gotta go!

Catch ya later,
Arbogast

Hunting Tips

From: Nougat **Nougat@e-meoww.com**
To: Arbogast **Arbogast@e-meoww.com**

Dear Arbo,

So, you're stalking spiders, huh? Personally, I don't like spiders much. They're too slow to be much of a challenge, they taste rotten, and some of them can hurt you, so watch out!

I've never understood how they can walk on the ceiling without falling off. I can't, and I'm pretty athletic. Oh well, we cats can do a lot more than dumb spiders, so let them go walk on the ceiling.

Don't get offended, kiddo, but I think it's time you sought out some more challenging prey. And if you can't find something, just make it up — I do it all the time. Just run around the house like you're chasing something, or something's chasing you. It's fun, believe me! It makes your folks think you're nuts, but what do you care?

> The more they don't understand you the more power you have. ***Practice being inscrutable!***

I've gotta catch a quick nap before dinner, so take it easy, kid.

Your wise uncle,
Nougat

Dinner is Served

From: Nougat **Nougat@e-meoww.com**
To: Arbogast **Arbogast@e-meoww.com**

Dear Nephew,

It has occurred to me that if you
want to continue **_purr_**-fecting your feline skills we need to cover the topic of
dining.

There are, I would guess, probably about 927 different kinds of cat food on
the market. Some of them are yucky but many of them are quite tasty. The
only way that you will be able to sample a whole lot of them is to practice
being fussy. This is not difficult. The greatest risk you run is having your folks
think "Well, if he's hungry he'll eat it eventually." This is a common obstacle,
but easily overcome if you've got a little stash of kibble stored away to get you
past those hunger pangs.

    Be finicky! While the yucky food sits there untouched by pussylips, just
mope around. Don't chase any toys or look interested in anything.

Pretty soon a different kind of food will appear in your bowl. Odds are it will
be more yummy than the last one. In time, your folks will find one you really
like. This will be good for a while, but then think of all those other flavors
you'll be missing…

Bon Appétit!
Uncle Noug

A Not-So-Excellent Adventure

From: Arbogast   **Arbogast@e-meoww.com**
To: Nougat   **Nougat@e-meoww.com**

Dear Uncle Nougat,

You sure are lucky you don't have a sister — mine gets me into more trouble!
Like yesterday, Lucie is whining and chattering to herself like she always does.

"I'm bored," she says. "Let's do something exciting," she says.

Every time she wants to do something we're not supposed to do, guess who
gets caught? You got it: **ME.** 'Cause everybody figures she's too dumb to have
been the mastermind!

Anyway, last night she comes up with the bright idea of a **BREAKOUT!** We
heard Mom coming in the front door and we just bolted! We didn't get very far
though. My stupid sister made it to the driveway where she hid under Dad's
car, and because I can't run as fast, I got nabbed on the front porch. We got
yelled at — Lucie was crying and crying — she's such a pussy! I toughed it
out though and tried not to look embarrassed... but I was.

Can you give me some tips on how to do it right? Besides ditching my dumb
sister, I mean. It's cool being an online feline!

Stay well Uncle Noug,
Arbo

The Great Escape

From: Nougat   **Nougat@e-meoww.com**
To: Arbogast   **Arbogast@e-meoww.com**

Dear Arbogast,

Sounds like you kids had a real ***cat***-astrophe! Here are a few things to keep in mind for future attempts:

1. Choose a nice day.
2. ***Make sure you eat first.***
3. Consider using a disguise.
4. Seeing as how there are two of you, take turns. One of you create a diversion while the other one breaks out.
5. And, of course, be sure you'll be able to get back in.

Another important thing you should arrange in advance is a good hiding place. You can create the illusion that you've broken out without going to all the trouble. Just when your folks are at the point of freaking out, you just sort of wander in. They'll be so happy to see you they'll let you do just about anything you want. It works for me!

Take care children,
Your Uncle Nougat

No Fleas Please!

From: Arbogast **Arbogast@e-meoww.com**
To: Nougat **Nougat@e-meoww.com**

Dear Uncle Nougat,

Hey, do you remember the other day when Lucie and me got outside?

Well, now my mom's all worried that we got fleas so she took us to **THE VET**.

I remembered what you told me about keeping my tail down, and now I understand why you told me that. But anyway, he gave mom these **HUMONGOUS** pills to give us.

There's no way those things'll fit down us! What shall we do?

Your nephew and his sister ("The Pill"),
Arbo and Lucie

Pill Tips

From: Nougat   **Nougat@e-meoww.com**
To: Arbogast   **Arbogast@e-meoww.com**

Dear Arbo,

Believe me kids, it was just a matter of time before your folks got on the flea pill kick. It's because they love you, of course, but also: they don't want to get bitten either. I've had a lot of experience with this and here's what you do when it's "that time of the month."

1. Hide. (Remember a while ago, I told you how important it is to have a really good hiding place?)

2. When they find you, look sad and pout — this has the added effect of clenching your jaws.

3. When they get your jaws pried open, and they stick the pill in your mouth, grab it with your tongue and tuck it inside your cheek. They will think you've swallowed it, and as soon as they leave the room you can spit it out someplace where they won't find it for a while.

4. When they find that pill, they will want to get it down you with renewed vigor. ***Repeat steps 1 and 2.*** This time they will shove the pill down your throat. But don't worry — we cats are equipped with a special thoracic muscle that, when exercised correctly, can eject any pill at warp speed. The pill is now nowhere to be seen, and the ritual will probably be postponed until next month.

Well kiddos, I gotta run.

Take care,
Uncle Nougat

Help! I'm Going Bald!

From: Arbogast   **Arbogast@e-meoww.com**
To: Nougat   **Nougat@e-meoww.com**

Dear Uncle Nougat,

I hate to keep bothering you, but something's going on that I just don't understand and I'm worried.

It all began a couple of weeks ago. I started noticing when I'd rub myself on something like a chair or my Dad's leg, some of my fur would stay behind. At first it was just a little, but lately it's like **CLUMPS**!

I sure don't want to go to **THE VET** again so I'm trying not to move around too much, so maybe my folks won't notice. But it's hard, you know?

What should I do, Uncle Nougat?

Please help!
Arbogast

You're Not "Losing It"

From: Nougat   **Nougat@e-meoww.com**
To: Arbogast   **Arbogast@e-meoww.com**

Dear Nephew,

What you are experiencing is called ***shedding***. It happens every year so get used to it. And don't worry about your folks taking you to ***The Vet***: it's not a serious condition. Actually, it can be kind of fun, so listen up!

1. This is an excellent time to test the "comfortability quotient" of your Dad's navy blazer or your Mom's favorite black dress.

2. If your coat tends toward the darker tones, stretch out on a clean, white bedspread or maybe an elegant ivory damask tablecloth! (This is especially effective ***just*** before dinner guests arrive.)

3. Another fun thing to do is to get comfy on something that you closely match, color-wise — something that people will sit on.

Watch the fun when they get up with their butts all covered with fur. Sometimes they don't notice until ***way*** later!

Have fun kids!

Fur-ever yours,
Uncle Nougat

Keep It Clean

From: Nougat **Nougat@e-meoww.com**
To: Arbogast **Arbogast@e-meoww.com**

Dear Arbo,

I cannot stress strongly enough the importance of good ***purr***-sonal hygiene. It is essential to a happy life. Believe me, if you don't do it for yourself, your Mom will do it for you. Even though I used to enjoy the great outdoors, if you're having fun, it is inevitable that some of the great outdoors will come in with you. And when that happens you will get a ***bath***.

I could go on at length about my experiences with the ***bath***, but I don't want to frighten you. Suffice it to say: one of the greatest advantages of living indoors is the resultant lack of need for the ***bath***. But I guess I wouldn't be a good uncle if I didn't at least give you guys a couple of pointers in case the need ever arises.

1. Hide. (They will find you — but it's always a good first step.)

2. Try to make yourself as flat and stiff as possible. Stretch out your legs and your tail like you've been run over by a truck. This makes it difficult for them to get you into the sink.

3. Once in the sink, try to get a grip — literally and figuratively. Your folks should know enough to place a bath towel on the bottom of the sink for you to hang on to.

4. Keep your eyes closed and your ears down. There's no need to add discomfort to your loss of dignity.

5. As soon as you get a good opportunity, ***run like hell!*** The wetter you are the better! Try to land on as many "Dry Clean Only" items as you can.

Well kiddos, try to stay out of hot water!
Uncle Nouggie

Company's Coming!

From: Arbogast **Arbogast@e-meoww.com**
To: Nougat **Nougat@e-meoww.com**

Dear Uncle,

We've got a serious situation here, Uncle Nougat. Our folks are getting the house all spruced up and we overheard last night that we're going to have **HOUSEGUESTS!**

We haven't had much company before — and never the kind that stays overnight. Usually Lucie and me just hide out until everybody goes home, but if people stay over and sleep in **OUR BEDROOM** what are we going to do?

Please hurry Uncle Nougat, I think they're almost here!
Arbogast

Being a Good Host

From: Nougat   **Nougat@e-meoww.com**
To: Arbogast   **Arbogast@e-meoww.com**

Dear Arbo,

I can't believe that you kids have avoided the scourge of houseguests this long! We have them a lot at my house. I guess that's the price you pay when you live near the beach.

Here are some tips to help you get through the ordeal. In fact, if you follow my advice closely you might put a damper on houseguests permanently.

1. ***Get out from under the bed and join the party!***

2. Understand that houseguests come in two varieties: cat ***lovers*** and cat ***haters***. Figure out which type you've got and act accordingly.

   CAT LOVERS: Ignore them. Eye them as you would a rancid sardine. Or better yet, don't make eye contact with them at all. Do not let them tempt you with anything. Be strong!

   CAT HATERS: Jump right up on their laps. If you get pushed off, get right back up there. Also, get especially cozy with the ones wearing clothes that contrast nicely with your fur. (Bonus tip: It's always a nice touch if you can manage to have a little tuna breath.)

3. Get involved in the food preparation, serving, and — most of all — eating.

4. When dinner starts, sneak under the dining room table and pass gas.

5. If you feel like throwing up, try to get up on the sofa as fast as you can. Or, if you can't manage that, find an open purse or suitcase. Even a bedroom slipper or shoe will do in a pinch.

Look at this as a great opportunity to hone some new skills!

Have fun kids,
Uncle Noug

Camera Shy

From: Arbogast **Arbogast@e-meoww.com**
To: Nougat **Nougat@e-meoww.com**

Dear Uncle Nougat,

My folks just bought a new camera and they're driving us
nuts trying to take pictures of us **ALL THE TIME**.

My dopey sister doesn't seem to mind, but I'm getting
tired of hiding under the bed.

Got any advice?
Arbo

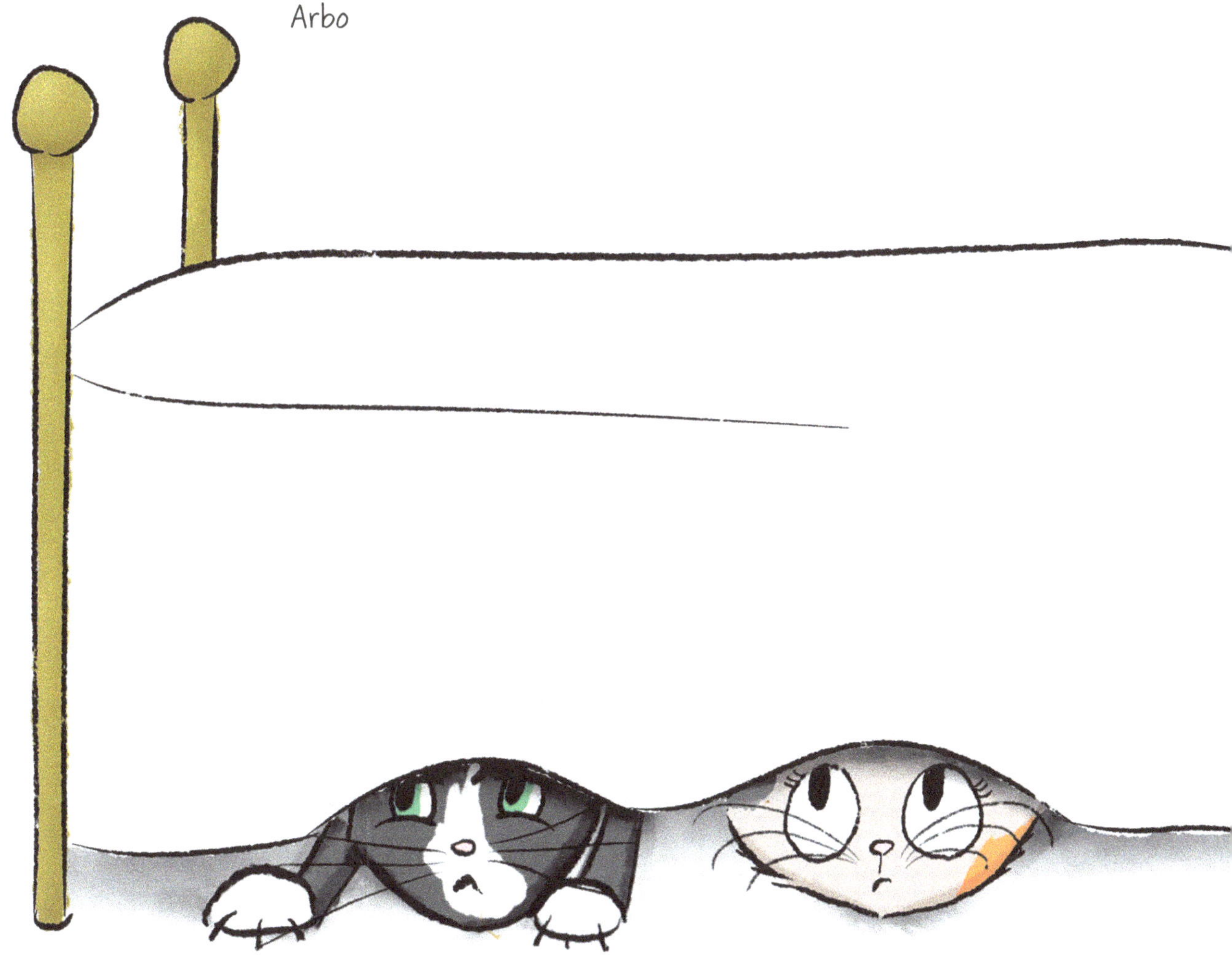

Thwarting the Photographer

From: Nougat **Nougat@e-meoww.com**
To: Arbogast **Arbogast@e-meoww.com**

Dear Nephew,

It is perfectly natural for your folks to want to take your picture. After all, what in the world is more photogenic than a cat?

Now, I can understand getting fed up with all the picture taking, but there's a way you can have a lot of fun with it, so listen carefully.

1. First off, it is vital that you let your folks capture **one** priceless photo of you doing something incredibly cute with relative ease. (This is what we call "the set up.") They will be so thrilled with the picture, they naturally will try to get more. And this is where your fun comes in…

2. When they are near you **without** the camera, strike a fantastic pose — like balancing yourself on one paw or dancing on your hind legs. Watch them scramble for the camera!

3. When they get back, ready to snap, just sit down and look stupid.

About once a year you'll need to let them get that **perfect picture** of you again to inspire them to keep on trying.

Say cheese!
Uncle Noug

Sleepless in Sacramento

From: Arbogast **Arbogast@e-meoww.com**
To: Nougat **Nougat@e-meoww.com**

Dear Uncle Nougat,

You remember those houseguests we got? Well, it looks like they're not going anywhere anytime soon.

The worst part is we got **EVICTED** from our room! They unpacked all their stuff in there, and every time they leave, they close the door so we can't get in. And my folks always keep their bedroom door closed! And to make matters worse they've got new slipcovers on the sofa and chairs and they're all covered in plastic. Yuck!!! When we jump up on them, we either slide off or our butts stick!

What do you think Uncle Nougat? Any suggestions? We really need our sleep!

Your tired nephew,
Arbogast

Clawstrophobia!

From: Nougat **Nougat@e-meoww.com**
To: Arbogast **Arbogast@e-meoww.com**

Dear Arbogast,

While it's cool to have your own room — I have mine of course — it's your right as a cat to be able to sleep *anywhere* you want to! From the sound of things, it seems to me that your best bet is to work on taking over your folks' bedroom. But first we need to solve your door problem. Here's what you do:

1. You will need to establish the rule in your household that *all inside doors must be kept open at all times.* In the meantime, you will have to learn how to open them yourself. Now, the level of difficulty depends upon the design of the door:

   The kind with the BENT HANDLE is the easiest to open. Just stand on your hind legs, reach up, and pull down the handle while putting your full weight against the door.

   The ROUND KNOB presents more of a challenge, but with practice — and both you and your sister working on it — you should be able to overcome this obstacle as well. Try standing on your sister's back to get some added height while you kind of roll along the top of the knob, and when you feel it move, you both push against the door as hard as you can.

2. Opening CUPBOARDS will be a snap once you have mastered your door skills. You never know what goodies might be lurking just the other side of *those* doors — like an economy-sized bag of kibble or other yummy stuff.

It is very important that you do not, under *any* circumstances, let your folks know about your new skills! You never know when you might want to use these techniques to help you get outdoors or someplace else they don't want you to go.

Keep me posted on your progress.

Good luck kids,
Uncle Nougat

What the Heck is Going On?

From: Arbogast Arbogast@e-meoww.com
To: Nougat Nougat@e-meoww.com

Hey Uncle Nougat,

Some really **WEIRD** things have been
going on around our house
lately. Like, almost every time my
mom goes out she comes home with big
bags of stuff. I don't know what the stuff is,
but the bags are very cool!

And then the other night my folks totally moved the
furniture around and all of a sudden there's this **HUGE
TREE** in the living room! But wait, it gets better!

Then they hung all these cool toys — round shiny ones
— on all the branches! But every time me or Lucie try to
knock them off or climb up the tree we get yelled at.

What's going on, Uncle Nougat? Are my folks losing
it? Should we be concerned?

Your nephew,
Arbogast

Merry Catmas Children!

From: Nougat **Nougat@e-meoww.com**
To: Arbogast **Arbogast@e-meoww.com**

Dear Arbo,

Ho, Ho, Ho! What you are experiencing, young nephew, are the preparations for a very special holiday: **Cat**mas (or **Puss**mas, depending on where you live). This is a celebration featuring the patron saint of pussycats — **SANTA CLAWS!**

Here's the drill:

1. It is important to write a good letter to Santa and send it early. Tell him what you want, like new toys, yummy stuff to eat, etc.

2. Be careful what you ask for. Once I included tuna on my list, and I ended up getting a whole case of it. (See my earlier note re: dining.)

3. Don't try to climb the tree or play with the ornaments **while your folks are in the room!** Wait until they go to bed, or better yet, until they leave the house.

4. If you happen to break something — and this is a good possibility — hide the evidence under the rug or behind the tree. By the time they find it, they'll think maybe it was an earthquake or something.

5. This is a good time to practice your people-food begging techniques. First, because there's an unusual amount of good eating during this holiday. Also, because it's the **Season of Giving**, at least at my house, my folks are a softer touch than usual.

Merry Catmas, children!

Your favorite uncle,
Noug

Merry Catmas Uncle!

From: Arbogast   **Arbogast@e-meoww.com**
To: Nougat   **Nougat@e-meoww.com**

Hey Uncle Nougat,

Thanks for clueing us in on Catmas. It sounds pretty fun except for one thing. Now you probably know this already, but Lucie learned a real important lesson the other day — **DON'T EAT THE CURLING RIBBON!**

Here's what happened… Lucie and me were home alone and having a swell time climbing in and out of the cool bags and playing around with the wrapping paper and ribbons. We were having lots of fun playing with the tree and everything, when all of a sudden, I noticed Lucie had a piece of curly red ribbon sticking out of her mouth. She looked pretty silly — like a pull-toy without the wheels — and she couldn't meow right. All she could do was squeak!

Of course, when the folks got home they freaked and tried to pull it out of her mouth. The problem was she'd swallowed about three feet of the stupid stuff and so she ended up having to go to **THE VET!** I told her what you told me about keeping her tail down and everything — but she didn't come home for days!

I never thought I'd be saying this, but as much as I complain about my sister I'm sure glad that everything "came out" OK. I sure missed her while she was gone.

Merry Catmas Uncle Noug,
Arbo

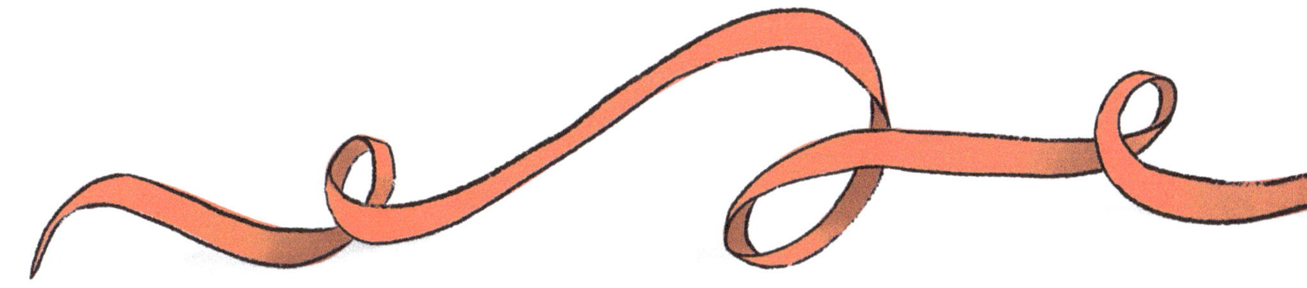

The Night Before Catmas
By Nougat

'Twas the night before Catmas and all through our house
not a creature was stirring, except for a mouse.

He'd entered my kingdom and run down my hall
(he must have got in through a hole in the wall.)

I peeked as he sat in the room with our tree,
a fat furry fellow who happened to be
just what I'd asked Santa Claws to send me!

I watched as he thought about what next to do,
and I pondered… "should I bake, broil or stew?"

My Catmas treat — so neat to eat —
I decided right then I'd begin with his feet.

Then all of a sudden there came a loud clatter,
he'd leapt on the table and upset a platter!

The next thing I knew I was hot in pursuit
of our tiny houseguest in his gray furry suit.

Then he darted for safety and to my surprise,
headed straight for our tree—with a gleam in his eyes!

As he ran up the trunk and perched high up on top,
he seemed to be taunting me! This had to stop!

A cat has his pride after all's said and done.
I had plans for this mousie — with some cheese, on a bun!

So I started up after him, slowly at first,
then quicker and quicker, 'til ready to burst…

I reached out to grab him! But just as I neared,
he flicked his tail sideways and suddenly veered

D
  O
    W
      N

the icicles hung from our tree with such care.
He landed with style and a great deal of flair!

Then he dared me to follow, which of course I should tell,
I did with much grace. But as the tree and I fell,

I decided this fellow had a certain appeal,
and he'd make a fun playmate instead of a meal.

Good Luck!